Elkhorn Slough

MARK SILBERSTEIN AND EILEEN CAMPBELL

MONTEREY BAY AQUARIUM®

Monterey, California

The purpose of the Monterey Bay Aquarium is to stimulate interest, increase knowledge and promote stewardship of Monterey Bay and the world's ocean environment through innovative exhibits, public education and scientific research.

Acknowledgements The authors would like to acknowledge the help of the Elkhorn Slough Foundation, the many people who supplied us with information and advice, and those who reviewed this manuscript for scientific accuracy, editorial exactitude and just plain enjoyability. Special thanks to John S. Oliver and Burton L. Gordon for their insight and inspiration.

Published in the United States by the Monterey Bay Aquarium Foundation, 886 Cannery Row, Monterey, CA 93940-1085.

Library of Congress Cataloging in Publication Data
Silberstein, Mark
Elkhorn Slough.

(Monterey Bay Aquarium natural history series) 1. Natural history—California—Elkhorn Slough. 2. Estuarine ecology—California—Elkhorn Slough. 3. Elkhorn Slough (Calif.) I.   Campbell, Eileen,   II. Title. III. Series.
QH105.C2S48 1989   508.794'76   89-14557

ISBN 1-878244-00-0

Photo and Illustration Credits:
Cover: Dugald Stermer
Andresen, Bette: 56 (bottom)
Blaisdell, Andrew C.: 59 (top)
Bucich, Richard: 36 (right), 39 (middle, bottom), 44 (top right), 56 (top)
Cailliet, Gregor: 14 (right)
Caudle, Ann: 9 (top right), 15 (right), 18 (top), 29, 30 (top), 31 (top), 32 (top and bottom), 33 (top), 35 (top), 36 (left), 37 (bottom right), 38 (left), 39 (top), 49 (bottom)
Cavagnaro, David: 26 (bottom right)
Elkhorn Slough Reserve Collection: 54, 62 (bottom)

Foott, Jeff: 15 (top), 20 (bottom), 27, 28 (right), 36 (middle), 47 (top right)
Hall, Howard: 32 (middle), 34
Hamlin, Roy-Ami/ Collection: 52 (right)
Harney, Michael/*The Ohlone Way* ©1978: 51 (top)
Jong, Christine: 17 (left)
Lanting, Frans/Minden Pictures: 14 (left), 47 (top left)
Mayer, Melanie: 10 (top), 20 (top), 25, 26 (top right)
Monterey Bay Aquarium: 5, 7, 16, 26 (middle right), 43 (bottom), 45 (top), 57
Moore, Ken/Dept. of Fish and Game: 22
Noonan, Robert: 4

Our Lady of Refuge, Parish, Castroville, Courtesy of: 51 (bottom)
Racicot, Craig: 8–9, 42 (top), 58
Rigsby, Michael: 19, 23, 28 (left)
Rountree, Thomas: 35 (bottom), 36 (top; bottom), 37 (top, left; middle right), 38 (bottom), 41, 44 (bottom), 45 (bottom), 62 (top)
Sea Studios, Inc.: 10 (bottom), 26 (bottom left), 30 (middle; bottom), 31 (bottom), 33 (bottom), 44 (top left), 48 (bottom)
Silberstein, Mark: 1, 9 (middle right), 11, 13, 17 (right), 18 (bottom), 26 (top left), 48 (top; middle), 54, 55

Slevin, L.S./Pat Hathaway Collection: 52 (top)
Stack, Tom/Tom Stack & Associates: 24
Vierra, Carlos/Courtesy of the Vierra family: 52 (left), 53
Webster, Steven K.: 9 (bottom right)
West, Larry: 38 (top right), 47 (bottom right), 59 (bottom), 61
Westmoreland, F. Stuart/ Tom Stack & Associates: 49 (top)
Wrobel, David: 15 (bottom)
Würsig, Bernd: 8 (top)

Series and Book Editor: Nora L. Deans
Designer: James Stockton, James Stockton & Associates
Printed in Hong Kong through Interprint, Petaluma, California

CONTENTS

Mists rise off the tide flats as the spring sun peeks over coastal hills. The sound of wind through beating wings is punctuated by a curlew's call. Three thousand sandpipers wheel and turn in unison, their white bellies reflecting the morning light in a brilliant flash. Another quick turn and the flock almost disappears, the birds' brown backs blending with the color of the mud flats.

The season of change is coming to Elkhorn Slough. Unseen by most visitors, fishes are moving into the shallow, protected waters from their winter homes in Monterey Bay and beyond. Stirrings of spring also reach the mud below. Lumbering sea hares, giants of the slug world, begin a ponderous courtship that will end with chains and circles of mating molluscs. On the marsh and mud flats, winter-dormant plants awake. The lifeless brown stems of pickleweed sprout new growth, and mats of bright green algae begin spreading along the channel edges.

At the mouth of the slough, a whistle breaks the early-morning stillness as boats slip out of Moss Landing Harbor and head for fishing grounds on the bay. These are mostly trawlers and gill net boats, only a small part of the fleet. Back in the harbor, restless crews rig the other boats for salmon; anticipation mounts as the season approaches. Above the harbor, the sentinel of the fleet roars—the Pacific Gas and Electric power plant. Its towers loom in curious contrast to the quaint harbor and the teeming tide flats. But then, Elkhorn Slough is a curious place.

1

SLOUGH BEGINNINGS

Elkhorn Slough sits on the central California coast about 100 miles south of San Francisco, in the middle of the curve of Monterey Bay. A narrow arm of the sea, it reaches inland, crooking north at the elbow and ending in a thin finger. Unknown to most visitors, this small embayment is adjacent to a huge underwater chasm—the Monterey submarine canyon. Stretching more than 25 miles out into the Pacific and more than a mile down from the water's surface, the Monterey Canyon could hold the Grand Canyon of the Colorado River.

First-time visitors expect to find a river associated with Elkhorn Slough. Its lower end looks like a river mouth, and its sinuous form is certainly riverlike. There is no river here today, but the slough is, in a sense, a fossil river. Perhaps as long as a million years ago, a sizeable stream flowed through this area to drain into the Monterey Canyon. On its way, it carved out the valley that is now the slough. At some point, movement along the San Andreas Fault to the east changed the course of the ancient river, leaving the slough as a blind-ending valley.

Elkhorn Valley remained a small drainage until about 15,000 years ago, when the last Ice Age began its thaw. As the great glaciers that covered Europe and North America melted back toward the poles of the Earth, their meltwater ran to the ocean, raising sea level hundreds of feet. The sea crept into Elkhorn Valley, refilling the ancient river course with salt water. Slowly, as sand and mud washed down from the uplands and accumulated in the valley, mud flats and then a saltmarsh began to grow along the margins. The current chapter of the slough's story had begun.

This chapter has seen many twists to the plot. The slough has retained its basic character, but has joined with both the Pajaro and Salinas rivers in various episodes, sharing with them its mouth to the bay. Both rivers have shifted their courses many times over history, flowing alternately through Elkhorn Slough or through mouths to the north and south.

In the slough's most recent history, human hands have been the agents of change. We've diked the marsh to hold back the tides, and rechanneled the streams, shaping the slough to fit our needs.

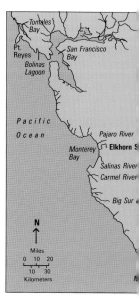

Monterey Bay's Elkhorn Slough boasts the largest extent of coastal wetlands between San Francisco Bay to the north and Morro Bay to the south.

From the air, Elkhorn Slough reveals many contrasting uses, from industrial plants at the mouth to open marshes in the upper reaches. The main channel is over seven miles long and is flanked by broad saltmarshes and rolling hills.

THE SEASONAL ESTUARY   What is a *slough* (pronounced "slew")? The best definition has a slough as a narrow, winding waterway edged with marshy and muddy ground. It can be salt water or fresh, open to the sea or apart from it. A slough is a type of *wetland*, a broader category that includes all types of land-plus-water environments. An *estuary* is a protected embayment with freshwater inflow from its land end and tidal exchange on its seaward side, where fresh and salt water mix. In simplest terms, it's an inlet where a river meets the sea.

Elkhorn is a full-time slough, but only a part-time estuary. Unlike San Francisco Bay, which drains the Sacramento and San Joaquin rivers, the slough has no year-round freshwater flow. With the winter rains, Carneros Creek fills with runoff from upper Elkhorn Valley and rushes down to empty into the slough. This infusion of fresh water can dilute the slough's saltiness to half that of the bay, a brackishness typical of estuaries. In spring, the creek slows, then dries up completely. The summer sun evaporates the still backwaters of the slough, concentrating them to a saltiness greater than sea water. Because of its winter-only freshwater flow, Elkhorn Slough is called a "seasonal estuary."

Tidal creeks meander through the marsh to the slough's main channel, as seen from an altitude of 500 feet.

Elkhorn Slough lies only 100 miles south of California's largest and most familiar estuary, San Francisco Bay. The slough is the largest coastal wetland between there and Morro Bay to the south, but its several thousand acres of tidal land would be dwarfed by many marshes in the world. Here on the Pacific Coast, where the land drops sharply off into the sea, most coastal wetlands exist only within the limited shelter of bays or other inlets. But along the country's sloping East Coast, long barrier islands buffer marshes that can stretch for miles along shore. And in the South, the Florida Everglades and Mississippi River delta wetlands spread across thousands of acres of wide, shallow plain as their rivers meander to the sea.

It seems there is no "typical" estuary—coastal wetlands are as different in character as in size and geography. Low-growing pickleweed is the most obvious plant at Elkhorn Slough, while eastern marshes luxuriate in waving seas of cordgrass and Florida's extensive swamps are shaded by cypress and mangroves. Coastal wetlands in the tropics and toward the world's polar regions have even less in common with our temperate estuaries. But estuarine wetlands do have similarities: anywhere in the world, you can look

Pickleweed, a hardy succulent plant, characterizes the slough's marshlands.

Elkhorn Slough's low-growing pickleweed marsh (left) contrasts with other coastal wetlands like this cordgrass marsh in Baja California (top), or this tangled Florida mangrove swamp (bottom).

for tide flats, waterlogged ground, salt- and moisture-tolerant plants, meandering waterways and wetlands wildlife.

You can also look for major cities on estuaries. Throughout history, people have settled in places where rivers meet the sea. Alexandria, Venice, Lisbon, Amsterdam, Calcutta, San Francisco— here and elsewhere, people took advantage of the access to inland and overseas trade, the rich soils deposited by the rivers and the abundance of fish, game and fresh water. Some of the world's busiest harbors were dredged from tidal creeks; some of its most productive farmlands were plowed from delta marshes, and some of its most intense industrial development has grown up at this interface of land and sea. Almost nowhere in the world are estuaries and their associated wetlands free from human influence.

In California, over 75 per cent of our original coastal wetlands have been entirely destroyed—dredged for marinas, diked off for pastures, or filled in for fields, buildings or freeways. In the process, we've lost thousands of acres of important fish and wildlife habitat. Even at Elkhorn Slough, one of the least-altered pieces of coastal wetland in the state, it's difficult to find a scenic view that doesn't include a building, fence, power line or plowed field. However, though humans have changed its face, the slough itself remains a vital and important coastal habitat.

The hand of humans is visible in some of the slough's remote corners. Today there's a harbor, industrial plants, agriculture, housing, roads and a railway.

THE VALUE OF ESTUARIES

Both pleasure and commercial craft find harbor in Moss Landing at the slough's mouth.

What good is a weedy, muddy old salt-marsh? "Not much, as it stands," was the answer of the past. Today the answer's not so simple. Between the findings of scientists and the changing perspective of the public, wetlands in their natural state have gained value. They're not just swampy wastes after all—in fact, wetlands can function as:

- Wildlife housing—many species of birds, mammals, fishes and invertebrates, including several endangered species, live only in coastal wetlands.

- Fish hatcheries—marshes are the favored breeding grounds for large numbers of fishes, including many commercially important species.

- Farms—saltmarshes grow more green material per acre than our best-managed farms, feeding a complex food web.

- Bird motels and diners—many migrating birds stop at marshes for food and rest on their long journeys.

- Tourist attractions—wetlands can bring in hunters, anglers, birdwatchers, boaters and other visitors, along with the money they spend in the local area.

- Job centers—wetland areas may provide jobs for tour guides, fishermen, marsh managers, and nature or sports store workers, among others.

- Flood and erosion control projects—many coastal marshes protect inland areas from flooding and destructive storm waves.

- Air purifiers—like any large expanse of green plants, saltmarshes absorb carbon dioxide from the air and release oxygen.

- Water treatment plants—water pollutants can be filtered by marshland soils, then absorbed by plants and soil organisms.

- Schools, laboratories, recreation centers and mental health retreats—we make direct use of wetlands by visiting them and studying their inhabitants.

Not all wetlands serve all these functions, and it's hard to pin an exact dollar amount on any of them. But the values are often great enough to compete head-on with potential income from development. Today when would-be developers ask, "What good is a weedy, muddy saltmarsh?" The answer is, "Add it all up—is your proposal worth as much as this wetland?"

2

SLOUGH HABITATS

If you started at the mouth of the Moss Landing Harbor in a small boat at low tide and rowed inland with the rising water, you'd get a look at all the parts that make the whole of Elkhorn Slough: the waterways, mud flats, marsh and surrounding uplands.

Imagine the journey . . . beginning outside the harbor mouth, your boat jostles as each wave rolls beneath it. On either side of you, the waves crash up onto the sandy beaches that flank the mouth of the slough. But ahead, the swells continue into Moss Landing Harbor, damping out as they move inland. You follow, floating past the two branches of the harbor, north and south, and up under the Highway 1 bridge. Beyond the bridge, Elkhorn Slough spreads out before you.

WATERWAYS The main channel of Elkhorn Slough is wide and relatively deep—700 feet across and 25 feet deep at its mouth. Even at the lowest of tides, there is water in this channel. It extends inland for seven miles, growing gradually narrower and shallower until it ends in a marshy expanse.

Past the first jog in the main channel, side streams begin emptying into it, cutting through the marsh to flow across the mud flats. At high tide these channels, called tidal creeks, fill with the incoming salt water. Like branching arteries, they carry tidal flow up into the farthest reaches of the saltmarsh, then reverse to drain it off as the tide drops.

Tides sweep in and out of the slough twice daily, bringing in clean bay water and flushing out silt-laden slough water. But the slough's long, narrow shape and lack of freshwater flow limit this exchange. The turning tide acts like a giant piston, compressing the ebbing waters and pushing them back to the slough's upper reaches before they can escape to the bay. These waters languish in the upper slough: it may take months for water there to be completely replaced with bay water, while in the lower slough it takes only days.

As a result of this discrepancy, the slough is almost like two bodies of water. The upper slough waters are saltier in summer and fresher in winter than lower slough waters; they're murky with suspended mud and nutrients; and surprisingly, they often have more oxygen due to masses of photosynthesizing algae.

Animals and plants respond to these differences. Toward the mouth of the slough, where exchange with the sea is greatest, oceanic species are abundant. As you move up the slough, backwater plants and animals are more common.

Low tide exposes acres of mud flats and empty tidal creeks (left). At high tide (below), you can paddle up the creeks through the marsh to groves of oaks.

An incoming tide brings clean salt water from the bay. In this aerial view, you can see the wedge of blue ocean water flowing from the slough's mouth at the top of the photo. It cleaves the rainy season's muddy water in the south and north harbors, at left and right, on its way upslough under the Highway 1 bridge.

Fishing at the mouth of the slough, you'd catch species that also live out in the bay: lingcod (above), halibut (far left and right), and some species of surfperch (left).

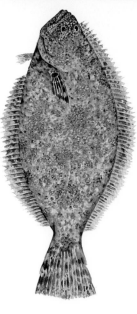

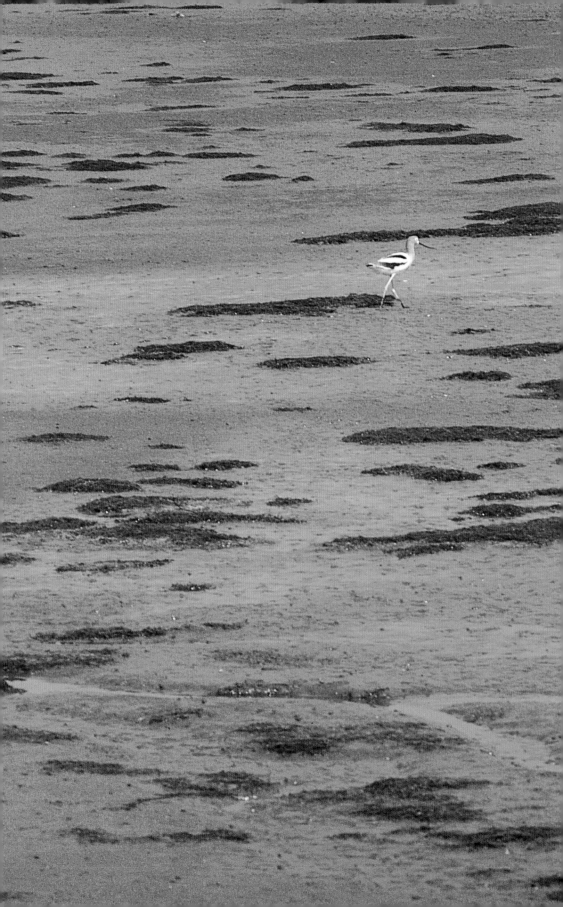

MUD FLATS Low tide exposes flat plains of mud between the water and the vegetation on both sides of the main channel. In the slow currents of the slough, fine sediments washed from the uplands drop out and settle, covering the bottom with layers of mud. Deposited over thousands of years, this mud may stretch down 20 feet or more. If you tried stepping out of your boat onto the flats of the upper slough, you'd find yourself thigh-deep in mud.

Even those most enthusiastic about the slough admit that the mud flats' charm is subtle. Their beauty is stark, like a moonscape; mud sucks at your boots if you try to explore, and what wildlife stays there goes below ground. To most people's eyes, the slough is more attractive when the tide is in and the flats are covered over, when the sky-catching water meets the green of the marsh without a belt of brown mud.

But to the eyes in the mud, the view is different. Crabs, shrimps, worms, snails, clams and others make a home here, digging into the soft sediment. The mud protects them from both animal predators and environmental extremes. They're washed twice daily by waters rich with food, and the sediment itself is so full of organic matter that many burrowers eat nothing but mud. Living on a mud flat does have its difficulties: lack of oxygen, gill-clogging silt and the periodic exposure to the drying air, among others. But the benefits are great enough that a single square foot of mud may be crowded with thousands of animals.

Mud crabs (below) live in mudbank burrows and come out to feed on algae. They keep a sharp eye out for danger, scuttling away sideways if threatened.

It takes a while to adapt to slough conditions. At left, a researcher tries to rescue his boot from the grasp of the mud.

SALTMARSH As the tide rises, you can steer your boat over to a tidal creek and follow it. You'll wind between pock-marked mud banks covered with pickleweed. The honeycombed banks are home to many burrowers, high-density housing that often crumbles from under the residents. Upstream, the creek grows narrower, until it's small enough to step over and the pickleweed carpet meets across the middle.

Here, you can pull your boat up to a mud bank and peer into the saltmarsh proper—the hundreds of acres of vegetation that are the next step upland from the mud flats. At Elkhorn Slough, this habitat is dominated by the succulent pickleweed (*Salicornia virginica*). The plant grows on former mud flats that have risen above the average reach of the tide. Pickleweed thrives on this higher ground, but the highest tides still swamp the marsh, leaving it too salty and wet for most other plants to tolerate. The marsh is

Saltbush

Salt grass

Pickleweed-crowned mudbanks become riddled with crab burrows and are heavily eroded by tidal currents.

spongy and springy with accumulated years of pickleweed tangle. The knotted mass hides and shelters its own community of animals: burrowing invertebrates like crabs and pill bugs, insects, birds, and small mammals like mice.

Where marsh meets mud flat, the tangle of root and stem catches mud, building up the flats and preparing them for future generations of pickleweed. But as the marsh advances on one front, it retreats on another. The building-up process eventually raises the marsh above the highest tides. The soggy soil drains dry and rain washes the salts out, making the ground fit for less-specialized plants.

This is the upper marsh, a transition area between marsh and uplands. Unlike in the lower marsh, where pickleweed grows almost uncontested, the upper marsh supports several species, including salt grass (*Distichlis spicata*), saltbush (*Atriplex* spp.) and alkali heath (*Frankenia grandifolia*).

Above the marsh, the land rises toward the hills. Technically, uplands aren't part of the slough, but the two are firmly linked: the hills contribute nutrients and run-off to the slough. The waterways moderate the climate and provide food for many upland animals.

UPLANDS In some places the transition from marsh to upland is gradual, and a weedy profusion of taller plants—wild mustard (*Brassica nigra*), coyote bush (*Baccharis pilularis*), berry bramble (*Rubus* spp.) and poison oak (*Toxicodendron diversilobum*)—replaces marsh species as you proceed upslope. But often hills rise so abruptly from the marsh that trees overhang the tidal creeks. The uplands are a wholly terrestrial habitat. Much of it is rolling grassy hills dotted with coast live oaks (*Quercus agrifolia*), or clustered groves of oaks shadowing a brushy undergrowth. The hills turn green with the winter rains, and in spring bloom with poppy, lupine and other wildflowers. Over the long dry summer, the hills bake to a golden hue, creating what many consider the quint-essential California landscape.

Rising above the marsh along the ocean end of the slough, a stretch of sand dunes creates a very different upland habitat. The

ridge of sand parallels the beach, sheltering the slough from ocean waves and blasting onshore winds. Because the dunes are so exposed, they're a difficult place for life to take hold. Like shifting, salty sand deserts, they support only the most tenacious plants. These pioneers settle the dunes, sending out long roots and runners that trap the sand like nets. They have much in common with desert plants: small fleshy leaves covered with fuzz or waxy skin to help conserve water, silvery colors to reflect the bright sun and an ability to thrive on few nutrients. In addition, they're able to survive salt spray and sandblasting winds.

Another challenging site is the sandy hills east of the slough. The soil here, made mostly of packed sand, is unable to catch or hold much of the winter's rains. Dry-adapted chaparral plants predominate. Manzanita (*Arctostaphylos* spp.), coyote bush, black sage (*Salvia mellifera*) and California lilac (*Ceanothus* spp.) form

The slough has several upland habitats, including sand dunes (above), oak-grassland hills (top left), and brushy areas covered by plants like poison oak (below left).

THE NON-NATIVES ARE RESTLESS

Hiking through the uplands at Elkhorn Slough, you pass through two different kinds of woodlands: groves of twisted coast live oak, then tall stands of eucalyptus trees. A variety of plants grows beneath the oaks: grass, shrubs, wildflowers, ferns. Birds and squirrels chatter; insects buzz. Under the leaf litter on the ground, you can scoop up a rich, earthy-smelling loam.

The eucalyptus grove has a different feel entirely. It's strangely quiet here; you see few birds or other wildlife. Nor are there many other plants. Long leaves and shreds of bark pile up beneath the trees, as if someone had abandoned their cleaning job.

The difference in feel touches on a debate that rages among conservationists. The oak trees are native Californians; the eucalyptus, immigrant Australians brought here in the mid-1800s as potential lumber trees. For many, eucalyptus trees are a symbol of the problems caused for native species by all non-native imports.

When a single plant or animal is removed from its native ecosystem and taken somewhere else, it leaves behind its predators, competitors, parasites and diseases. Freed from such natural checks and balances, and with a corresponding advantage over the natives in its new land, its numbers can explode. Many non-native plants spread like weeds, shouldering out native species to grow in nearly pure stands.

The new species are often not as useful to other plants and animals as the natives they replace. The eucalyptus tree's camphor-laden leaves and bark discourage insects and other browsers, and poison the ground for other plants. Soil organisms can't break the litter down after it has fallen. With no insects to feed upon, few birds live in eucalyptus groves. Many non-native species like eucalyptus reduce the diversity of plant and animal life where they grow.

Because of this, many conservationists advocate removing plants such as pampas grass, Scotch broom, ice plant, hemlock and eucalyptus, and replanting with natives. But

Eucalyptus trees, native to Australia, have become naturalized around Elkhorn Slough. While they eliminated habitats for some native plants and animals, they provide resources for others, like these roosting cormorants.

several plans to remove eucalyptus groves have triggered public outcry. A tree is a tree, say many, even if it doesn't "belong" here. Nectar-feeders like bees and hummingbirds do frequent eucalyptus forests, and monarch butterflies, herons, egrets and raptors will roost there.

With non-native species, the choices aren't easy and the trade-offs may be great. But we have to decide which we value more: a tree in the hand, or several native species that might live in the bush.

a thicket impenetrable to most large mammals, but cozy and safe for large numbers of birds, rodents and reptiles.

Like dune plants, chaparral plants grow small, leathery, gray-green leaves, the drab uniform of drought-resistant vegetation. Even when they bloom, the performance is subdued: their flowers are generally small and unshowy. To find what's most striking about chaparral plants, you have to use your nose instead of your eyes. Many of them produce pungent smells—a discouragement to deer and other browsers, who prefer their food unspiced.

Other slough uplands support a different dominant species. A common and spreading resident, its habitat is characterized by cultivated fields, salt ponds, industrial plants and houses.

Dense stands of tough chaparral plants cover the sandy hills east of the slough.

3

SLOUGH INHABITANTS

Your journey through the slough carries you through rich habitats teeming with life.

PLANTS Many of the slough's plants are obvious, but others look like nothing but a golden sheen on the mud or a murkiness in the water. These are tiny one-celled plants called phytoplankton, including diatoms and dinoflagellates. They thrive in the slough's waterways, where nutrients and sunlight are abundant.

Large algae also favor the slough. In the spring, a stringy green alga (*Enteromorpha intestinalis*) grows to cover most of the upper mud flats in the slough, turning winter's bare mud a luminous green. High tides often lift these algal mats from the mud and deposit them in veils over the upper marsh. In late summer, these bleaching mats blanket the shore. The red, spaghetti-like alga (*Gracilaria lemaneiformis*) also becomes luxuriant in the spring. In good years, it carpets the lower mud flats with tangled strands and masses.

Algae need to be wet to live. Left high and dry, they die. Most flowering plants, on the other hand, can't live with even their roots beneath water. An exception in the slough is eelgrass (*Zostera marina*), which grows in clumps on the mud at or below the average low tide. Like land-bound grasses, eelgrass puts down roots and grows seeds, but does it all below water. Because it's a solid presence in a swirling world, eelgrass becomes the center of a small community: shrimps and worms burrow in the root-bound soil, pipefishes lose themselves among the waving blades and various species festoon it with their eggs.

Across the mud flats and above the average high tide level, pickleweed spreads in a thick icing across a mud plateau. If one plant characterizes Elkhorn Slough, it is pickleweed. Little more than juicy, jointed stems with flowers so small they're almost invisible, pickleweed looks like a stringy, weedy cactus. This resemblance isn't accidental. As far removed as a swampy salt-marsh seems from a hot, dry desert, plants living here face similar challenges. With water everywhere, there's still not a drop to drink.

Salty water draws fresh water out of roots like a sponge, causing most plants to wilt and die. Pickleweed solves this problem by being saltier than the water it grows in. In effect, it becomes the sponge, drawing water in. Taste the plant's bulbous sections and you'll find they're natural pickles. Pickleweed stores the extra salt in its branch tips. In fall, the stems turn a rosy red to crimson, then wither and

The diatom (above, shown 200 times life-size) is one of the most important of estuarine plants. Diatoms and larger algae (right) feed the base of the slough's food web.

In the slough's calm waters, algae like Enteromorpha (above left) and Gracilaria (below left) grow luxuriously. The tide deposits floating mats of Enteromorpha on the upper shore where it bleaches a ghostly white. As these algal mats decompose, they provide food for invertebrates.

Pickleweed blooms in the spring (top) with tiny flowers. In fall, its succulent stems turn red (middle and bottom), then fall off, leaving only dried brown stems over winter. The broad ribbons of eelgrass washed up on a rocky shore (right) were once much more common in the slough.

drop off, taking the stored salt with them. In spring, green stems sprout anew from the rootstalk, free from the previous year's burden of salt.

Other marsh plants employ different methods for living on brackish water. Instead of storing salt, salt grass secretes it. Look closely at its narrow blades and you'll see small white crystals—salt the plant has sweated out through special pores. Salt grass grows a step above pickleweed's turf, in a tough mat of roots and runners that further stabilizes the marsh's soil.

In the summer, you might see the marsh draped with what looks like orange cobwebs. This is dodder (*Cuscuta salina*), a parasitic plant that takes root on pickleweed and other plants, robbing them of moisture and nutrients.

Oddly, one plant that is prominent in saltmarshes throughout the temperate zone—cordgrass (*Spartina foliosa*)—is absent from Elkhorn Slough. In East Coast marshes, cordgrass grows in wide swaths, making its own zone between mud flats and pickleweed. This zone is flooded daily by tides. Cordgrass survives in the soggy, airless soil by sending oxygen down to its roots through special gas-transporting tissues. Cordgrass doesn't grow in the slough. No one's quite sure why; apparently cordgrass needs some specific conditions to survive that just aren't present in the slough.

INVERTEBRATES In the marine environment, animal species without backbones outnumber vertebrates by more than twenty to one. In the slough, invertebrates float through the channels, hide in the algae and attach to solid objects—but mostly, they burrow in the mud.

Salt excreted from the pores of salt grass (left) crystalizes on the blade into the characteristic square salt shape. Rain will wash it away. The yellowish flowers (above) belong to the parasitic orange dodder, not the pickleweed beneath.

The best-known inhabitants of this undermud world are
the clams. Clams use a muscular "foot" for digging down into the
mud, then send up a "neck," or siphon, to the world above. The
siphon is actually two tubes, one that sucks in water carrying food
and oxygen, and another that spews out water carrying wastes.

The clomp of a footstep causes a clam to pull in its siphons
and clam up tight. If you come seeking clams, watch for a spout
on the mud flat. When the gaper clam (*Tresus nuttallii*) is dis-
turbed, it squirts a yard-high jet of water into the air. Look down
to find its siphon hole; stick your finger in and you can feel its
two-foot-long neck retract into the mud. Sunburst tracings on the
mud around a smaller hole show how a white sand clam (*Macoma
secta*) used its long, flexible siphons to vacuum for a meal. Clams
with shorter siphons—or no siphons at all, like the basket cockle
(*Clinocardium nutalli*)—live close to the surface of the mud. The
cockle often lies above the surface, but can burrow out of sight in
seconds.

Not all holes in the mud lead to a clam. If the hole is round
and surrounded by a cylindrical sand collar, you've found the digs
of the fat innkeeper worm (*Urechis caupo*), also called the weenie
worm. Both names are apt—the rotund pink worm shares its
U-shaped burrow with an assortment of boarders, including two
types of crabs, a worm, a small clam and a little fish.

Another digger that shelters guests is the ghost shrimp
(*Callianassa californiensis*). These shrimp excavate a branching
tunnel system. To ventilate their home, they scull constantly with
special fanlike legs, moving clean water through the maze. Once
abundant in the slough, ghost shrimp have been so heavily

*Looking beneath the
surface, you can see how
different clams can be.
From left to right, these
are gaper, Washington,
bent-nosed, littleneck,
cockle and geoduck
clams.*

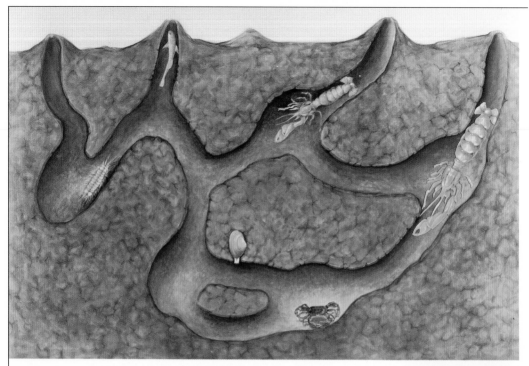

harvested for bait that few are left. (Bait-hunters don't even have to dig for the shrimp; they just suction them out with special plungers.)

Worms abound in the slough. In fact, a single shovelful of mud would probably contain several kinds, from the threadlike rubber-band worm (*Notomastus tenuis*) to the dragonlike, five-foot-long clam worm *Neanthes brandti*. Sometimes the worms are so closely packed that a dug-up chunk looks like a root ball come squirming to life.

At high tide, snails stoically plow the surface of the mud. Some are peaceful harvesters feeding on algae; others are predators looking for prey. Snails without shells—sea slugs—also glide singlefooted through the slough. The sea hare (*Aplysia californica*), named for its humped shape and earlike antennae, also shares its namesake's vegetarian tastes. Hiding in *Gracilaria* algae and eating 10 per cent of its weight in algae per day, a young sea hare can grow from a half-inch size to a foot-long, 12-pound adult within nine months.

Mud crabs (*Hemigrapsus oregonensis*) scuttle along the flats, and their cousins the shore crabs (*Pachygrapsus crassipes*) peek from burrows higher in the mud banks. These creatures are often so abundant they cover the mud with a solid layer of crabs. The bank-dwellers share the neighborhood with a burrowing pill bug (*Sphaeroma quoyana*), and other burrowers live among the pickleweed. Both the marsh and the slough uplands are home to a host of flying and crawling insects.

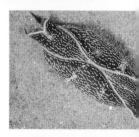

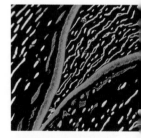

This predatory sea slug (middle and bottom), is the "bloodhound" of the slug world. It tracks molluscs by following slime trails, then swallows its victims whole.

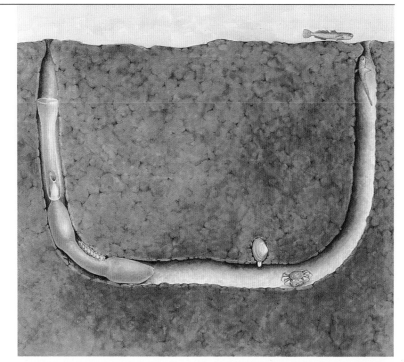

Both ghost shrimps (left) and fat innkeeper worms (right) shelter other species in their burrows. The sign of the inn is easy to recognize: the worm forms a cylindrical collar at one end of its hole (below).

FISHES As the tide rises over the mud flats, fishes from the deeper channels surge in for the feast. The bat ray (*Myliobatis californica*) glides along just above the mud, stirring up a wing-wide swath of sediment that unearths clams and other burrowers. It can also pop fat innkeeper worms out of their lodgings, using its wings like a plumber's helper. Bat rays crush their hard-shelled prey with a mouthful of broad, flat "pavementlike" teeth.

Other rays and a number of sharks feed along the slough's muddy bottom, rooting up burrowing invertebrates, or sometimes just snipping off exposed clam siphon tips. The leopard shark (*Triakis semifasciata*) is the largest of these—up to seven feet long. To fishes and bottom fauna, it's a fearful predator, but human visitors to the slough needn't worry: its teeth are small and its nature timid.

Flatfishes feed along the bottom, and also from within it. Some shuffle down into the mud, like hens settling on their eggs, until all but their eyes are buried. Then they wait, ready to lunge up and grab unwary fishes passing overhead. Others grub in the mud for buried and hidden prey.

Few fishes live year-round in the slough's upper reaches, where the concentrated salinity of summer waters is diluted to brackishness by winter rains. The staghorn sculpin, or "bullhead," is one of

Flat-shaped fishes like the bat ray (above) and the buried flatfish (left) usually live on or near the bottom. The bat ray has a weapon in that sharp spine near the base of its tail. The flatfish relies instead on its ability to hide in or on the bottom.

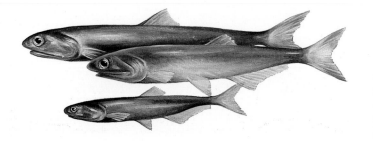

Anchovies swim in schools of thousands of fish, and are often eaten by many other slough animals.

the most common backwater fishes; it hatches, swims, eats and mates in the slough. It also steals bait from hooks, much to the dismay of anglers. But the bullhead can make a unique replacement bait: strong, sharp spines on its gill covers turn the sculpin into a living fish hook.

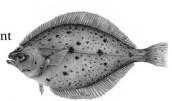

Another full-time resident, the bay pipefish (*Syngnathus leptorhynchus*) doesn't live on the mud as many slough fishes do. Nor does it assume their usual mud-colored disguise; instead, it often is bright green or brown. The green is like neon against the mud, but when this blade-shaped fish plants itself in a clump of eelgrass, it all but disappears.

Silvery schools of midwater swimmers—Northern anchovies (*Engraulis mordax*), Pacific sardines (*Sardinops sagax*), Pacific herring (*Clupea pallasi*) and topsmelt (*Atherinops affinis*) and jacksmelt (*Atherinopsis californiensis*)— are also better camouflaged than might appear at first glance. To predators below, their silver bellies blend with the bright surface waters, while to a bird's eye, they present drab-colored backs. Swimming in schools is also a defense, since it's hard to single out any one fish. But the schools themselves draw predators; they're "baitfish" for our fishing fleet and a natural target for diving birds, seals, sharks and other large fishes.

Camouflage is a matter of shape and behavior as well as coloration. Flat sanddabs (top) and staghorn sculpins (above) lie quietly on the bottom, while long, thin pipefish (below) plant themselves tail-down and wave like strands of sea grass.

SLUGS ON YOUR NERVES

The sea hare releases a cloud of purple ink as a defensive act.

What do you do with a ten-pound slug? The California sea hare (*Aplysia californica*) seems to have few redeeming qualities. This lumpy sea slug isn't warm and furry, or noble, or impressive. It isn't edible, either by people or by other marine animals because its body contains noxious chemicals that presumably taste bad. It also secretes large quantities of mucus. If asked, most people would probably dismiss the sea hare as a lowly, gross and slimy animal. From the human point of view, this seems to be a creature with no reason to exist.

But as the worm turns, so does our story. Sea hares currently fetch $10-15 apiece on the open market, and tens of thousands have been sold over the past few years. In fact, the demand for these saturnine slugs has been so great that it spawned one of the most profitable and longest-lived mariculture operations in Elkhorn Slough: the Sea Life Supply Slug Ranch.

These improbable animals are the centerpiece of some of the most advanced neurological research happening today. Sea hares possess some of the largest nerve cells in the animal kingdom, some reaching nearly a millimeter in diameter. The large nerve cell size, combined with the sea hare's relatively simple behavior, allows scientists to study connections between the actual nerve cells and animal behaviors.

With researchers demanding a steady source of slugs, New York's Columbia University developed a way to hatch and rear the animals from eggs. But California sea hares need West Coast algae, and the cost of importing it soon got out of hand. So Elkhorn Slough's Sea Life Supply got the job of rearing the sea hares to usable size.

Columbia hatched the eggs and started the baby slugs, sent them west for fattening, then flew them back east for the researchers there. That's a lot of trouble for a "worthless" slug—but not for an animal that aids in understanding how animal, and ultimately human, nervous systems work.

Walking along the mud flats at the mouth of the slough, you might find a sea hare stranded by the tide. If you do, stoop down and place it back in the water—a small acknowledgement of the major understandings its kind has given to ours.

What other discoveries and cures might be lurking in the slough's muddy waters? What implausible species might hold the keys to future scientific breakthroughs? If we value them all, and protect their lives and homes, we'll maintain the opportunity for future discoveries.

BIRDS The slough is a tight patchwork of subhabitats, where birds of water, marsh, field and forest live virtually side by side. Over 250 species of birds inhabit the slough or its immediate surroundings for at least some part of the year.

On the main channel, brown pelicans (*Pelecanus occidentalis*) dive from above to scoop fish into their pouches, while loons (*Gavia* spp.), cormorants (*Phalacrocorax* spp.), grebes and diving ducks make their fishing forays from the water's surface. Mallards (*Anas platyrhynchos*) and other dabbling ducks turn tail-up in the shallows to search for edible greenery.

In shallow water at the channel's edge, a snowy egret (*Egretta thula*) stalks a fish, sharp beak ready to dart and grab. Its startling white catches the eye; in contrast, a great blue heron (*Ardea herodias*) looks like a weather-grayed fencepost, faded against the water. The large, exotic-looking blue herons are actually quite common in the slough and since 1985 have nested each spring high in a nearby grove of pines.

When low tide lays the mud flats bare, thousands of shorebirds flock to the spread. From a distance, the birds are indistinguishable, their feeding indiscriminate. Closer, you can pick out many species—some with longer legs, some with shorter or sturdier beaks, some large, some small. They all feed on the flats, but each species has a specialty. Black-bellied plovers (*Pluvialis squatarola*) scan the surface with their large eyes, then pick up morsels with their short beaks; marbled godwits (*Limosa fedoa*) use their six-inch bills to probe for deeply burrowed prey; avocets (*Recurvirostra americana*) wade in with their long legs and sweep the water for food.

Above the mud flats, secretive birds like the endangered clapper rail (*Rallus longirostris obsoletus*) hide in the marsh vegetation. The clapper rail lives its whole life among the pickleweed. It almost never flies; instead, it runs away from danger, dodging through the tangle, or stands still and hides. Though the rail is seldom seen, its clacking call can sometimes be heard echoing across the water. Smaller birds—sparrows, blackbirds, swallows—also make a home in the marsh, or visit to nibble plants, catch insects, or rest in the shelter of a pickleweed screen.

Upland Elkhorn Slough is itself made up of many habitats: grassland, oak and eucalyptus groves, brushy chaparral, dunes, farms and suburban yards. Each has its own roster of birds, from coveys of California quail (*Lophortyx californicus*) in the brush through barn swallows (*Hirundo rustica*) to backyard garden songbirds. You might see a hovering kestrel (*Falco sparverius*) ready to strike, or the hunched, watchful shape of a red-tailed hawk (*Buteo jamaicensis*). A pair of golden eagles (*Aquila chrysaetos*) breeds in the slough uplands, and endangered peregrine falcons (*Falco peregrinus*) hunt in the slough as they pass through on their migrations.

Many of the waterbirds that live in the slough dive for their dinners. The Western grebe, red-breasted merganser and common loon (above) dive from the water's surface to catch fish below.

The northern harrier (below) scans the marsh and grasslands for rodents, and captures them in a quick dive from the sky.

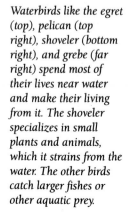

Waterbirds like the egret (top), pelican (top right), shoveler (bottom right), and grebe (far right) spend most of their lives near water and make their living from it. The shoveler specializes in small plants and animals, which it strains from the water. The other birds catch larger fishes or other aquatic prey.

Shorebirds like dowitchers (top), black-necked stilts (left), avocets (above) and willets (right) fan out onto beaches and mudflats at low tide. Some use their long, thin bills to tweeze burrowing crabs, worms and snails from the mud. Others, like the avocet, snatch up food lying above the mud.

Songbirds find food and shelter around the slough. The black phoebe and the marsh wren (above) feed on insects. Both the wren and the red-winged blackbird (right) nest in rushes and cattails.

The clapper rail (right) is well-adapted to marshy habitats: a narrow body and flexible wings help it move through dense vegetation; long toes keep it from sinking in the mud. But because the rail is so specialized, its numbers have declined as wetlands disappeared. It's now considered an endangered species.

MAMMALS, REPTILES AND AMPHIBIANS Mammals, too, frequent the slough. Harbor seals (*Phoca vitulina*) loll on the low-tide mud flats, safe from approach by land or by sea. One wallow is a particular favorite; seals haul out there so often that locals have dubbed it "Seal Bend." California sea lions (*Zalophus californianus*) and sea otters (*Enhydra lutris*) also swim in from the bay, but usually stay near the harbor mouth, where you can often see them from the Highway 1 bridge.

Red-legged frog

You'll see nothing of most other mammals but their tracks: baby-like feet and forepaws mark the path of a raccoon (*Procyon lotor*); long, narrow hindpaw prints show where a rabbit (*Sylvilagus* sp.) crossed; tiny hieroglyphic skitters were left by a mouse or maybe a shrew.

The mice of the marsh nibble on pickleweed segments and build their nests in pickleweed branches. And when the highest tides wash over the marsh, they cling to the tops of pickleweed strands, where they make an easy meal for hawks and owls. Larger mammals—opossums (*Didelphis marsupialis*), skunks (*Mephitis mephitis*), deer (*Odocoileus hemionus*), red fox (*Vulpes fulva*), coyote (*Canis latrans*)—live in the slough's upland areas.

Pacific pond turtle

Snakes and lizards also frequent the uplands, generally avoiding the wetter areas of the slough. Turtles, frogs and newts, including the endangered Santa Cruz long-toed salamander (*Ambystoma macrodactylum croceum*), gather along the creek flowing into the slough or around the area's freshwater ponds.

California newt

Sea otters (right) swim in from the bay and feed on clams within the slough. Harbor seals (below) spend much of their day sunning on the mud, returning to the water when the tide covers the flats.

4

CYCLES IN THE SLOUGH

Estuarine saltmarshes grow more green matter per acre than a
Kansas cornfield, a level of productivity that supports tremendous
numbers of animals. Almost two-thirds of the fishes and shellfish
caught each year in this country are species that spend at least part
of their lives in estuaries.

One of the keys to this great productivity is the meeting of land
and sea. Water running into estuaries from the land contains
minerals dissolved from rocks and organic nutrients washed from
the soil. Water from the ocean contains its own mix of minerals
and nutrients. Combined in an estuary, each supplies ingredients
missing in the other. The slough waters, sloshed back and forth
by the tides, let the nutrients steep long enough for the plants to
make full use of the super-mix. Fertilized by land and sea, slough
plants thrive.

Diatoms and other phytoplankton—microscopic, single-celled
plants that form the "pastures of the sea"—occur in such numbers
that they color the slough waters greenish-brown. In peak seasons,
millions of these floating plants can inhabit a single quart of water.

Pickleweed covers hundreds of acres in the slough. Few animals
feed directly on pickleweed or other marsh vegetation, but as the
plants die and decompose, their fragments provide food for count-
less protozoa and bacteria. These microscopic decomposers and
micro-grazers, suspended in the slough's water along with the bits of
rotted plants, make a rich soup called detritus. Invertebrates such as
worms, clams, shrimps and amphipods feed on this soup. Some use
feathery filters to rake it from the water along with the diatoms;
others gather it from the mud.

The thick algae mats that lie everywhere also contribute to the
soup. In West Coast estuaries, especially those studied in southern
California, the decayed algae seem to be the most important
ingredient in slough soup.

These plants form the first strands of the slough's food web,
converting energy from the sun into edible form. As invertebrates
slurp the soup, the original solar energy begins making its way
through the slough food web: the filter-feeders are eaten by small
fishes; the small fishes by larger fishes and birds; the larger fishes by
seals, sharks or human beings; and eventually bacteria return us all
to nutrients that the plants can use, beginning the cycle again.

Snowy egrets nest in the spring. Beautiful, airy plumes are part of their breeding plumage. After nesting season, they'll molt and lose the long, decorative feathers.

Through summer and fall (top), the grass-covered hills dry to gold and the marsh turns green as pickleweed sprouts new growth. In winter and spring (above), rain turns the hills green, while the marsh is brown.

SEASONS Though visitors from elsewhere in the country might find them hard to recognize, California's central coast has distinctive seasons. Three seasons, in fact.

Weather in coastal California is dominated by the influence of the Pacific Ocean. Not only does the ocean moderate the climate, but the coast's seasons cycle with the oceanic year. In spring and summer, northwesterly winds blowing down the coast conspire with the Earth's rotation to drive coastal surface waters offshore. Colder water from below wells up to take its place ("the upwelling season" is the name for spring and summer in the lingo of local oceanographers.)

When warm, moist winds blowing from the ocean meet cool coastal upwelled water, moisture condenses into cool gray fog. (That's why shivering summer visitors to "sunny California" head for the sweatshirt vendors.) The slough itself sits at the mouth of a funnel for the deepest, coldest water around—that from the Monterey Canyon—and so may get even more than its fair share of summer fog. The fog bank may stop very near the shoreline or can extend several miles inland. On some days Moss Landing Harbor is shrouded in fog, while the upper slough is warm and sunny.

If disappointed tourists stayed into early fall, they'd catch the best weather of the year. The northwest winds die down and cease to pump cool water from below; warmer waters return from offshore; the seas are calm and the fogs disperse during this "oceanic season."

After October, the winter rains begin. Storms blow in from the Pacific, hitting the coast before sweeping east across the rest of the continent. Between winter storms the weather is clear and cool. Almost all of the slough's rain falls between November and March, when the northwest winds begin again.

SEASONAL CYCLES: REPRODUCTION AND MIGRATION In the slough, as elsewhere, life cycles are tied to the cycle of the seasons. Springtime brings more than fog. The upwelled waters, rich in nutrients, fertilize marine algae, which burst into bloom. They turn the coastal waters into murk and carpet the slough's mud flats with green.

Fishes take advantage of the abundant food and mild weather to breed. Many coastal species migrate into the slough, a favored nursery for young fishes. Some, like herring and topsmelt, attach clusters of eggs to rocks, algae or eelgrass. The plainfin midshipman (*Porichthys notatus*) excavates a nest under a rock, and makes a humming noise to attract a mate. The female lays eggs on the rock, which the male fertilizes and guards until they hatch. Others, like leopard sharks and bat rays, give birth to live young in the slough's tidal creeks. Anchovies simply release their eggs into the water, where they float with the tide as the larvae develop.

The adult fishes soon return to the sea, but many of the young linger in the slough's protected, food-rich waters until fall, growing larger and less vulnerable. Then they, too, migrate into

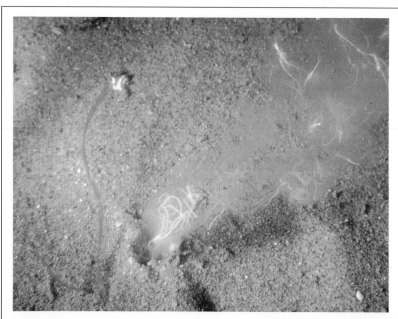

Innkeeper worms spawn in the spring (left). Deer grow antlers in preparation for fall mating. The sandpiper (below) makes a yearly migration of thousands of miles to lay eggs and raise its young.

the bay to feed and grow before returning to the slough and continuing the cycle. This seasonal influx of fishes is invisible to us, but the birds know: terns and pelicans flock to the summer slough and plunge from the air to feed on these schools of fishes.

Fishes come and go, but the invertebrates are always here. Indeed, those stuck in the mud can't even emerge to mate. Instead, they sow their seed, spewing eggs or sperm out into the water, perchance to meet and be fertilized. The larvae resulting from such meetings are on their own, and the vast majority never make it to adulthood. Of the millions of eggs released by a female clam in her life, almost none will survive to release its own eggs.

This scattershot approach is typical of invertebrates that live near the mouth of the slough, but many of those in the slough's backwaters have a different strategy. Here, where extremes in temperature and salinity are the norm, the young need extra nurturing. Certain worms, amphipods and a tiny mollusc called the gem clam (*Gemma gemma*) hold onto their eggs, brooding them until they hatch and the young leave home. The pea-sized gem clam may shelter in its shell a dozen or more young, each the size of a grain of sand. Though these animals have fewer offspring, the care they lavish ensures that more will make it to adulthood.

Great blue herons, common slough residents, feed along the shore and marsh. These stately birds nest in tree tops near the slough.

Other invertebrates mate and lay eggs. Sea hares are hermaphroditic—each is both male and female. They can't fertilize themselves, but several animals can mate at once, each acting as male to the one in front and female to the one behind. Biologists have described complete "Roman circles" of mating molluscs. Each sea hare then lays large masses of yarnlike strands containing up to a million eggs. Twelve days later, the eggs hatch into swimming larvae that settle to the bottom to become slugs. Fortunately, predators eat most of these larvae—otherwise, the planet would soon be knee-deep in purple slugs.

Spring in the slough is also a season of birds. One spring day in 1983, a group of birdwatchers stood at a spot overlooking the slough and counted 116 different species of birds—to this date, the most ever seen in North America from one spot in one day. In the spring and again in the fall, tens of thousands of migratory birds stop at Elkhorn Slough on their journey along the Pacific Flyway, the migration route for West Coast birds. Shorebirds like black-bellied plovers, long-billed curlews (*Numenius americanus*), and Western and least sandpipers (*Calidris mauri* and *C. minutilla*) use this route for a seasonal commute that may take them from Arctic summer breeding grounds to tropical wintering areas. For these birds, Elkhorn Slough is a critical stop for resting and feeding along the way.

As birds wing their way overhead on thousand-mile journeys, the Santa Cruz long-toed salamander inches along underfoot, intent on its own migration. As the rains begin at the end of fall, the salamanders make their way to freshwater ponds near the slough. They breed and lay their eggs in the ponds, then return to their woodland homes.

MIGRATION

If you're a birdwatcher, Elkhorn Slough in the summer can feel like a resort town in the wrong season. While fall and winter virtually vibrate with birds—flocks of hundreds and thousands of sandpipers, dunlins, dowitchers and other shorebirds—summer finds the slough quiet except for the "locals" like pelicans, terns and gulls.

But if you lived high in subarctic Alaska or Canada, your birdwatching year would be in full swing. By June, hundreds of thousands of shorebirds, ducks, geese and other birds arrive on the tundra's boggy thaw. Like human jet-setters, they're drawn by sunshine, food and the lure of sex. The Arctic's frenetic two-month summer, with its 24-hour daylight and explosion of insects and other food, makes it the ideal place to find a mate and raise a quick clutch of young.

But by late August or September, the insects die off, the bogs and ponds begin to freeze up and the birds head south again. Some fly non-stop, but most make the trip in stages, traveling along broad routes called flyways. They stop at specific sites to rest and feed, then continue onward.

Some will fly over 3,000 miles, down to South or Central America; others settle in at Elkhorn Slough and other West Coast locations for the winter. Even those that don't make it any farther than California log more flight miles in a year than most of us who watch them. That little sandpiper you see down on the mud flats, the one you consider one of our common local species, is really an exotic traveler. If it could talk, it might tell of frozen tundra plains bursting into bloom or of mangrove-lined Costa Rican beaches.

What does Elkhorn Slough have to do with these diverse wetlands? All are critical to migrating birds. Each prairie pond, river delta or coastal saltmarsh they stop at through the year can be vitally important to their safe arrival at the next spot. Shorebirds at Elkhorn Slough depend on the health of places you may never see.

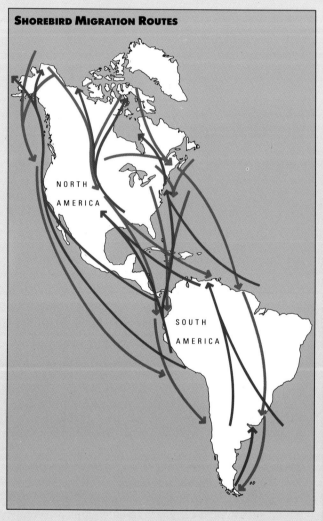

SHOREBIRD MIGRATION ROUTES

NORTH AMERICA

SOUTH AMERICA

The trans-hemispheric life of these birds is recognized by the International Migratory Bird Act and other cooperative ventures aimed at preserving both the birds and their habitats. Because these birds have no nation, the people of all nations must join in responsibility for their survival.

Nocturnal animals are like a "second shift." They play similar roles to daytime creatures: when mudflat-feeding shorebirds go to roost, raccoons (below) take up the search for invertebrates, and leave behind evidence of their wanderings.

DAY AND NIGHT Seasonal change is only one of the cycles that affects slough residents. The coming of night or the ebb of the tide can set animals in motion. Though their movements may be measured in feet instead of miles, these migrations are as important as a shorebird's yearly flights.

As night falls, the slough's cast of active characters changes. Raccoons lumber softly out of the woods to forage at the marsh's edge. Footprints in the mud reveal their rounds, and droppings full of shell bits betray their taste for snails and crab. Opossums, skunks and owls are also creatures of the night, their movements familiar to slough watchers who stay up late.

Along the sandy shore at the mouth of the slough, beach hoppers (*Orchestoidea californiana*) make nightly forays to wave-cast piles of flotsam, algae and other organic debris. They scavenge efficiently for edible bits, incidentally helping to keep the beaches clean. Visit the beach at night and you can catch them in a flashlight beam, orange antennae shining. By day you won't see them, they burrow into the moist sand above the tides.

The hordes of hoppers attract nighttime predators such as burrowing owls (*Athene cunicularia*) and occasional shorebirds, who arrive to dine on the unwary.

TIDAL EBB AND FLOW The tides ebb and flow twice daily in the slough, lagging behind those in the bay by 45 minutes at the slough's upper end. The range between the highest high tide and the lowest low tide is about eight vertical feet, a distance that uncovers many horizontal yards of mud flat when the tide is out.

The intertidal is a world in flux; first wet, then dry. Those living here can cope with both, but the tidal cycle rules their lives. As the tide ebbs and exposes mud flat and shoal, the creatures of the slough take refuge. Fishes retreat into the depths of the main channel or wait out low tide in burrows or pools. Mud-flat invertebrates like worms and clams withdraw into tubes and holes; crabs dig down into the mud for protection. Snails pull into their shells and seal the opening to keep from drying out until the water returns.

At high tide, multitudes of phoronid tube worms (*Phoronopsis viridis*) send their tentacles up from the mud to filter the overlying water for food. There are often so many small green crowns that they color the bottom like a field of moss. As the tide ebbs, the worms pull their delicate tentacles down into sturdy tubes of cemented sand grains. Invisible on the drained mud flat, they're protected from drying and safe from predators.

The slough looks like two places at high and low tide (top and middle). While the tide's in, filter-feeding animals like the phoronid worms spread their tentacles to feed (above).

The moon snail (*Polinices lewisii*) is another of the creatures tied to the tides. At high tide it hunts through the mud, searching for the scent of clams. When it finds a clam, the snail surrounds it with a huge, fleshy foot and begins to drill into the shell. Using its filelike tongue, the moon snail rasps a countersunk hole, then feeds upon the flesh within. Empty shells found on the flats will often reveal these telltale holes.

Many birds are also tidal clock-watchers. Shorebirds that feed on burrowing invertebrates wait for the ebbing tide to expose their mudflat cafe. As the water drops, they flock from roosting sites in the salt ponds or upper marsh and descend upon the flats. The best place to feed is just above the receding water: burrowers there are still close to the surface and haven't had a chance to pull down into the mud. As the tide continues to ebb, the birds move up the slough to flats that are just being exposed.

Plants grow and die; animals come and go; days and tides and seasons change. The patterns are predictable, but as they overlap and interweave, these cycles create ever-shifting scenes in Elkhorn Slough.

A flock of sandpipers (top) waits for the ebbing tide to uncover the mud flats. Moon snails, like the one above, bury themselves in the mud to wait out low waters.

5

PEOPLE AND THE SLOUGH

Since entering the scene at Elkhorn Slough, humans have directed much of the action. They've shaped the set as well, each different culture modifying the environment to suit its needs. The slough you see today is the product of all these changes.

Though people probably lived in the slough as long as 10,000 years ago, the earliest culture that left evidence was that of the Ohlone (pronounced "oh-**lone**-nee") Indians, also called the Costanoans or coast people. As long as 4,000 years ago, small tribelets inhabited the coast from Point Sur to San Francisco Bay. They roamed the slough and Monterey Bay for thousands of years, the longest-lived culture in the area's history. But today, beyond a few spare accounts by early European visitors, we know them only by evidence dug from the ground. Mounds of broken shells and bones—garbage dumps from the past—have given us clues to the Ohlone diet. Recent excavation of an Elkhorn Slough village site showed archaeologists how the local Indians lived; a nearby cemetery, how they died.

The slough was a rich and varied resource for these people. In addition to fishes, shellfish, game and edible plants, it supplied materials for making tools, clothing and shelter. The Ohlone used stone or bone to make scrapers, mortars, awls, fishing sinkers and other tools. They wove local plants into baskets, made clothing from skins, and adorned themselves with colorful feathers and shells.

What little they needed from outside the area, they got through trade. Their knives and arrowheads were chipped from chert or obsidian, two hard, glassy stones that give a sharp edge. The nearest source of chert is Point Año Nuevo, 50 miles to the north; their obsidian came from Napa County and from the eastern slope of the Sierra Nevada.

Camped in the groves of oaks along the shore, the Ohlone fished the slough's waters, hunted marine mammals, stalked deer and elk and trapped birds and small game. They gathered acorns, seeds and other nutritious plants. And they feasted on the slough's shellfish. Indeed, they may have feasted heavily enough on one species to severely thin its numbers.

In a shell mound excavated near the village, archaeologists found abundant shells of the native oyster (*Ostrea lurida*) in the bottom layers—the ones laid down longest ago. Higher in the mound—more recently in time—the oyster became scarce and was replaced by clam species common today: gapers, cockles, little-necks and others. Did the Indians overharvest the oysters, or did

For thousands of years, Ohlone people harvested the slough's bounty (left). The painting below, from the late 1870s, shows the Salinas River flowing past a ferry at the mouth of the slough; you can see both Moss's landing and the railway that took away much of its business. A budding Castroville is visible in the left center while Toro peak flanks the right side of the Salinas Valley. The painting now hangs in a church in Castroville.

the shellfish decline due to natural changes in the slough's environment? The answer remains to be discovered by future archaeologists.

The Ohlone controlled their environment in other ways. They set fires to keep shrubby vegetation from overrunning the open grassland where large game grazed and useful plants grew. At times, the smoke from these fires was thick enough to obscure the sun. Grasses soon sprang back to cover the ashes, but the slow-growing coastal scrub was kept at bay.

The Spanish took this fire-clipped landscape from the Ohlone Indians when they began settling missions in the 1700s. In the hundred years of their reign, the Spanish altered the central coast landscape more than it had been changed during centuries of Ohlone occupation. Spanish cattle, roaming free over the oak-covered hills, grazed the native bunch grasses and tromped them into the dust. Non-native grasses took their place, accidentally imported as seeds on the cattle and in the fodder brought to feed them. Other foreign plants escaped from fields and gardens, and together with the grasses changed the face of the environment.

The coming of the Americans in the mid-1800s further modified the landscape. Ambitious farmers and ranchers drained marshes in the lowlands and along river mouths and turned the extra acreage over to pastureland and crops. Loggers stripped the hillsides of trees. Whalers put out from the shore of Moss Landing to capture migrating

From the mid- to late 1800s and again in the 1920s, whaling (above) was a major bay industry. The port built by Charles Moss (below) saw a brisk traffic of tall-masted ships (below left).

whales, and a processing plant onshore reduced the giant mammals to oil and whalebone. Charles Moss, full of plans and schemes for his town at the mouth of the slough, built shipping facilities and a pier to accommodate the water traffic he hoped to attract.

For a while, Moss's plan seemed headed for success. From the mid-to late 1800s, Hudson's Landing at the head of the slough served as Watsonville's port. Farmers from the Pajaro Valley and surrounding areas brought their grain and produce to the slough and loaded it on flat-bottomed boats. At high tide, the boats sailed down the slough to Moss Landing, where the produce was trans-ferred to coastal schooners bound for gold-boom San Francisco. Even a stern-wheeled steamboat, the *Vaquero*, plied the slough's waters at the height of its prosperity.

But Moss's dream was derailed in 1872 by the coming of Southern Pacific, which built its main rail line from San Francisco along the edge of the slough. Today, the train rumbles directly past the old site of Hudson's Landing, close enough to shake what remains of the piers.

The slough still supported a variety of local businesses. Just after the turn of the century, several groups began farming oysters. The Vierra family, early slough pioneers, grew oysters, ran a ferry service, built the first bridge across the slough, and diked off a few hundred acres of the marsh for salt evaporating ponds. These ponds, abandoned since 1974, have become the most important pelican roosting area north of Point Conception. Ironically, this

Around the turn of the century, the pioneering Vierra family diked a large area of wetlands for harvesting salt. Evaporation concentrated the brine in a series of ponds, finally drying it to salt. Workers harvested salt with shovels and wheelbarrows.

roosting ground was threatened when a dike broke in 1982 and returned the natural tide flow to the ponds.

Elkhorn Slough has had various re-plumbing jobs in its history. Originally, the Salinas River joined the slough near its mouth before they both flowed into the bay. Sometime around 1908, farmers re-routed the river. They dug a new channel to the bay through the dunes south of Moss Landing, and put up tide gates to keep the river from its old path. Deprived of freshwater flow, Elkhorn Slough became a tidal embayment, saltier and less estuarine than before.

Industry lives alongside plants and wildlife at Elkhorn Slough. This is "Mighty Moss," the PG&E power plant at the mouth of the slough.

The slough remained a quiet backwater through the first World War, but began waking up as World War II dawned. In the 1930s, an active and prosperous oyster-growing industry made Elkhorn Slough the second-largest supplier in the state. The salt ponds provided salt for local fish canneries, which processed tons of sardines and other fishes into cheap protein for a nation at war.

Heavy industry came to the slough in the early 1940s, when Kaiser Industries built a factory at Moss Landing. The plant, now called National Refractories, extracts magnesium from sea water and makes it into heat-resistant bricks used in high-temperature ovens. In 1950, the Pacific Gas and Electric Company (PG&E) built a steam-generated power plant nearby. Expanded in 1967, "Mighty Moss" became the second-largest plant of its kind in the state. Today, this plant supplies the power needs of much of central and northern California. Its twin stacks, 500 feet tall, are landmarks visible from around the bay.

In 1946, the Army Corps of Engineers made the biggest plumbing change in the slough with the construction of Moss Landing Harbor. Where formerly the slough had wound north before emptying into the bay, the Corps cut a straight-shot channel through the sand dunes, and piled rock jetties to keep it in place. Moss Landing Harbor was built both north and south of the new channel, with facilities for vessels of many sorts. Today it harbors a commercial fishing fleet of over 400 boats, 200 pleasure boats and a growing sportfishing contingent. The north harbor, home of the Elkhorn Yacht Club, has launched many a Pacific cruise.

For almost as long as entrepreneurs and engineers have been shaping the slough, scientists have been studying it. In the 1920s, George and Nettie MacGinitie of Stanford University conducted the first ecological study of a California estuary here. Ed Ricketts, author John Steinbeck's buddy and the model for "Doc" of *Cannery Row*, collected specimens from the slough's rich waters. Generations of scientists and students have traveled from Stanford, Berkeley, San Francisco, San Jose and farther afield to study the slough.

In 1966, the California State University system began operating Moss Landing Marine Laboratories. The Labs focus a great deal of attention on the slough. Continuing this tradition of research in Elkhorn Slough, two new research centers have recently been formed. The Monterey Bay Aquarium Research Institute explores the canyon beneath the bay. The Elkhorn Slough National Estuarine Research Reserve sponsors scientific research as well as programs for schools and the public.

MARSH RESTORATION

Several hundred acres of diked marshlands had been used as pastures since the 1940s.

Today, researchers are studying the populations of marsh animals returning to the restored marshlands.

Our grandfathers and grandmothers acted on the best information and used the best methods of their time to dike and drain marshlands, converting them into productive grazing or croplands. Today, with new information about the value of wetlands as wildlife habitat, we're again using the best methods available—but this time we're reclaiming for nature the lands our grandparents once "reclaimed" for economic uses.

Restoring a marsh to its original state is not as simple as breaking the dikes. When marshland dries after being removed from tidal influence, the soils shrink and collapse. Reflooding creates a shallow lake instead of a marsh. This was the situation in 1983 when the California Department of Fish and Game decided to return several hundred acres of Elkhorn Slough's diked marshlands to the tides. The area, used as pasture for nearly 40 years, had subsided as much as three feet below the level of the undisturbed marsh. Before opening the levees, workers dredged a channel through the pasture and used the dirt to create small mounds and islands that would rise above the water.

With the return of the tidal flow, fishes and invertebrates soon moved back to the site. Within two years, the new marsh's animal populations were almost identical to those of the slough. Plants took longer to colonize, but today most of the islands and mounds have a cover of pickleweed. Birds returned, too, and over 100 species now use the area.

Scientists from Hopkins Marine Station in Pacific Grove are working on another restoration project, attempting to restore eelgrass to Elkhorn Slough. This plant was once extremely abundant in the slough, covering dozens of acres of tide flats. Today it grows only in small patches, due possibly to the turbidity and erosion caused when the harbor was opened in 1946. Researchers have had good success so far, and with some luck we may once again see waving strands of green gracing the slough's waterways.

Similar efforts to restore wetlands and other habitats are underway throughout the country. Some have been more successful than the Elkhorn Slough projects, some less. Overall, it's clear that we still have much to learn. But it's also clear that with a little help from us, nature can begin to heal itself; that restoring degraded habitats can be as important as conserving pristine ones. Much of this work is done by local groups and individuals who've realized the value of their native landscapes. By working in our own backyard, we can make a difference to our planet.

6

ELKHORN SLOUGH: TODAY AND TOMORROW

If you want to explore Elkhorn Slough, a good place to start is the Visitor Center located east of Moss Landing off Elkhorn Road. Part of the Elkhorn Slough National Estuarine Research Reserve, the center has exhibits and information on the slough and is the starting point for five miles of trails. The reserve is managed by the California Department of Fish and Game in conjunction with the National Oceanic and Atmospheric Administration. Research, education and interpretive programs on the reserve have been developed by the Elkhorn Slough Foundation, a non-profit organization dedicated to the conservation of Elkhorn Slough and other coastal wetlands.

From Kirby Park on Elkhorn Road, you can follow a trail that parallels the marsh and offers good birdwatching. This is part of a several-hundred-acre wildlife preserve owned and managed by The Nature Conservancy. (The Nature Conservancy is a national land trust that in the early 1970s became the first of several groups to acquire Elkhorn Slough land.)

For a visit to the ocean end of the slough, turn off Highway 1 north of the bridge for Moss Landing State Beach, which is managed by the State Department of Parks and Recreation. Here, the sea meets dunes and the dunes meet marsh. On the beach side of the dunes, anglers can surfcast for lingcod, rockfishes, surfperches and other species. You can also fish from the rock jetty protecting the harbor mouth. In winter, surfers gather off the beach to catch the big waves that roll in from Pacific storms. Inland a bit, walk north along the strip between the dunes and Bennett Slough and you'll follow the former route of the Salinas River and Elkhorn Slough. This is one of the best places in the area to watch migrating birds; you're bound to see many kinds of shorebirds and waterfowl.

The Moss Landing Wildlife Area is another good birding spot. The wildlife area, located a mile north of Jetty Road along Highway 1, is the newest access to the slough. It boasts four miles of trails and two wildlife viewing blinds.

South of the slough's mouth, the town of Moss Landing offers restaurants and fish markets for hungry visitors. Its main business is fishing, but Moss Landing is also home to several antique stores and to Moss Landing Marine Laboratories.

You can also explore the slough by boat. Two public launch ramps give access to the slough. At the mouth, the yacht club has a large-boat ramp. In the upper slough, at Kirby Park, you can launch smaller craft, especially canoes and kayaks. If you go boating in the

Elkhorn Slough serves many people: fishers (top), hikers (bottom), boaters, birdwatchers and anyone who wants to dig in and discover.

THE SLOUGH UP CLOSE

How can you get a real good, close-up look at the slough's most intriguing wildlife without resorting to shovels, scuba or strong binoculars?

Visit the Monterey Bay Aquarium, about twenty miles south of the slough. An exhibit modeled on Elkhorn Slough gives you cutaway views through the mud, revealing ghost shrimps in their branching tunnels and fat innkeeper worms at home with their various guests. You'll see how buried clams lie with their siphons extending like periscopes to the surface. You can pick out pipefishes from look-alike blades of surfgrass.

Out through a set of revolving doors, another "slice of the slough" recreates a walk from the slough's saltmarsh across the dunes to the beach—a half-mile hike compressed to 65 feet. Ruddy ducks paddle on a section of tidal creek while flatfishes and leopard sharks cruise below. Windows let you peer through water much clearer than the real slough "soup."

The scene rises to a sandy dune where plovers and sandpipers scamper. You'll have to resist the temptation to reach out and touch the birds, they're so close. Hatched and raised in captivity for the most part, the birds seem totally unconcerned by your presence. On the other side of the dune, small waves lap on the beach. Surfperches and other fishes swim "offshore," rolling with the water motion.

The aquarium experience lets you see what lives below the mud, under the water or hidden in the pickleweed. In all, the aquarium exhibits a small fraction of the number of species of fishes, invertebrates, birds and plants that actually inhabit the Elkhorn Slough. But it's enough to whet your appetite for a visit to the real place, where there's more to see than meets the eye.

The aquarium's aviary exhibit gives you a bird's-eye view of the slough.

slough, be sure to check the tides to avoid stranding on shoals or mud flats exposed at low tide.

When's the best time to visit the slough? Certainly the seasons will affect what you'll see. For birdwatchers, spring and fall are the high-volume seasons, as tens of thousands of birds pass through on their annual migrations. But in winter, many shorebirds and waterfowl use the slough, and birds like pintails (*Anas acuta*) are only here in this season. In summer, pelicans return from breeding in Mexico and southern California. Flying in long squadrons, they commute out to the bay to feed during the day, then return to the slough to roost.

June is the slowest month for birders, as most of the migratory birds are on their northern breeding grounds. But June brings sharks and rays into the slough to breed, and visitors can often catch a glimpse of these animals as they cruise the shallow waters for food or mates. Wildflowers bring color to the slough in May and early June, while pickleweed takes up the palette in fall to tint the marsh a rosy hue.

Whether you come for research, recreation or just a quiet walk, in winter, fall, summer or spring, this small pocket of diversity will always have something to show.

Elkhorn Slough is one of the few places in the world where you can stand in the shade of an oak and see shark fins cutting through the surface of the water. If you visit in summer, you'll see brown pelicans (bottom).

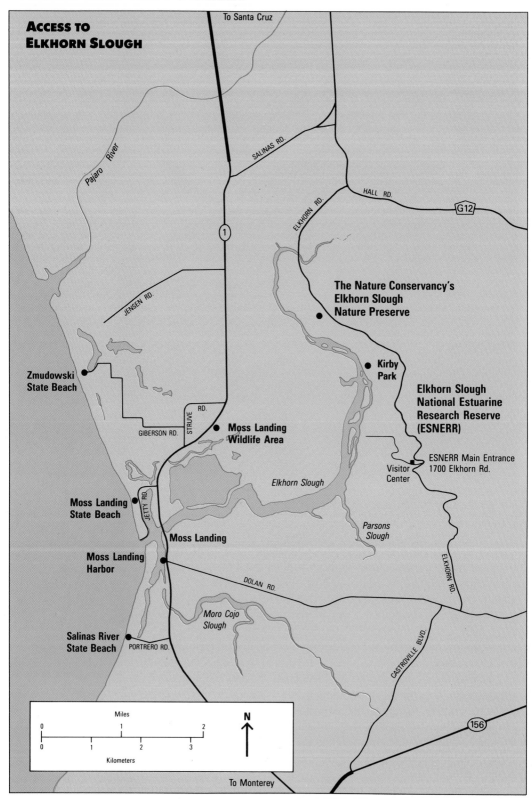

Many organizations and agencies cooperate to preserve the slough environment. You can visit the slough from a number of different access points shown on the map above.

TOWARD TOMORROW Boating up a tidal creek tucked into the hills, your view of Elkhorn Slough is much the same as an Ohlone Indian's would have been 3,000 years ago: water, marsh, birds and blue sky. But around the next bend, PG&E's twin towers thrust into view. A Forster's tern (*Sterna forsteri*) hovers like a white flame, unconcerned by the Amtrak train on its daily run below. Snowy plovers lay their eggs on crumbling salt pond levees. The slough is full of such contrasts, evidence of a history shared with humans.

Its history of change continues today. The channel of the slough grows wider and deeper each year, scoured by tidal currents flowing through the altered harbor mouth. Once-common species like ghost shrimp and eelgrass have become rare. Clams and shellfish, though still abundant, take up so much coliform bacteria and pesticide runoff from the hills above the slough that health authorities warn they shouldn't be eaten.

Other pressures loom, among them potential land-use conflicts from a growing population that needs more housing, farmland and better roads.

Coastal wetlands across the world have long felt the pressure of human proximity. They've been viewed as a resource to be developed—something with little intrinsic value, but much potential. In southern California, the quiet marshes of San Pedro were transformed into the south's largest harbor and industrial port, leaving the curlew's call only a memory. In Florida, thousands of acres of the Everglades disappeared; conservationists still battle for water rights to sustain what remains. Around San Francisco Bay, growing cities pushed out onto the marshes, diking or filling until less than a quarter of the wetlands were left. Other wetlands succumbed to similar fates.

But in the 1960s, as more city dwellers with more leisure time grew to value wilderness for its escape value, news stories about air pollution, DDT and vanishing species began to shock people into environmental awareness. Attitudes started to change: no longer was the local saltmarsh just a weedy swamp waiting to be made useful; it already worked as wildlife habitat, open space and a dozen other functions that could be weighed against its development value.

The public's increasing awareness and appreciation of the multiple values of wetlands spawned an array of government and private programs to acquire, preserve, protect and manage this resource. In 1972, the federal government enacted the first nationwide wetlands regulatory program in Section 404 of the Clean Water Act and focused increased attention on coastal wetlands by passing the Coastal Zone Management Act. A number of state and local governments have passed wetlands protection legislation as well. At all levels of government, both public and private protection and management of wetlands has been established.

Elkhorn Slough has benefited from these changes. In the early 1970s, The Nature Conservancy bought 400 acres of the slough

The Everglades, like many coastal wetlands, faced many threats from human development but are now being protected as valuable wildlife habitats.

and set it aside as protected habitat. Since then, state and federal agencies, private groups and individuals have acquired over 3,600 additional acres to preserve the slough and its inhabitants. People have also begun reversing the changes of the past. In 1983, slough managers breached a tide gate built 40 years earlier and restored the tidal flows to 400 acres of land. Populations of burrowers have now reclaimed the flats and pickleweed is growing on the higher ground.

Elkhorn Slough has accommodated many uses in its history: hunting, agriculture, fishing, recreation, industry, education, research and residential housing. Human pressures on the slough and other coastal wetlands are likely to increase even further as more and more people move to the coast. By the year 2000, it's estimated that over 75 per cent of the United States population will live within an hour of the sea or the Great Lakes. Despite protective laws and regulations, hundreds of wetland acres a year still fall to development. It is a testament to the slough's vitality that it thrives amidst these pressures. It will be a test of our commitment to see that it and other wetlands continue to thrive into the future.

Elkhorn Slough shelters a number of threatened and endangered species, including least terns, which nested here in the past (above), sea otters, brown pelicans, Santa Cruz long-toed salamanders and clapper rails.

To learn more about the slough and what you can do to help protect it, write to the Elkhorn Slough Foundation, P.O. Box 267, Moss Landing, CA 95039.

A SAMPLING OF ELKHORN SLOUGH SPECIES

Plants
Alkali heath *Frankenia grandifolia*
Blue-eyed grass *Sisyrinchium bellum*
Coyote bush *Baccharis pilularis*
Eelgrass *Zostera marina*
Eucalyptus *Eucalyptus globulus*
Field mustard *Brassica campestris*
Filaree *Erodium cicutarium*
Fleshy jaumea *Jaumea carnosa*
Manzanita *Arctostaphylos* spp.
Meadow barley *Hordeum brachyantherum*
Poison hemlock *Conium maculatum*
   oak *Rhus diversiloba*
Pickleweed *Salicornia pacifica (virginica)*
Poppy, California *Eschscholzia californica*
Oak, coast live *Quercus agrifolia*
Sage, California *Artemisia californica*
Salt grass *Distichlis spicata*
Soap plant *Chlorogalum pomeridianum*
Sticky monkeyflower *Mimulus aurantiacus*
Toyon *Heteromelea arbutifolia*
Wild radish *Raphanus sativus*
Willow *Salix* sp.

Invertebrates
Clam, gaper *Tresus nuttallii*
   white sand *Macoma secta*
   gem *Gemma gemma*
Cockle, basket *Clinocardium nutallii*
Crab, mud *Hemigrapsus oregonensis*
   lined shore *Pachygrapsus crassipes*
Fat innkeeper worm *Urechis caupo*
Ghost shrimp *Callianassa californiensis*
Geoduck *Panope generosa*
Moon snail *Polinices lewisii*
Mussel, bay *Mytilus edulis*
Oyster, Pacific *Crassostrea gigas*
Phoronid tube worm *Phoronopsis viridis*
Sea hare *Aplysia californica*

Fishes
Anchovy, Northern *Engraulis mordax*
Bat ray *Myliobatis californica*
Bay pipefish *Syngnathus leptorhynchus*
Flounder, starry *Platichthys stellatus*
Goby, arrow *Clevelandia ios*
Halibut, California *Paralichthys californicus*
Herring, Pacific *Clupea harengus pallasii*
Lingcod *Ophiodon elongatus*
Longjaw mudsucker *Gillichthys mirabilis*
Sanddab, speckled *Citharichthys stigmaeus*
Shark, gray smoothhound, *Mustelus californicus*
   leopard *Triakis semifasciata*
Sole, English *Parophrys vetulus*
Staghorn sculpin *Leptocottus armatus*
Surfperch, black *Embiotoca jacksoni*
   pile *Damalichthys vacca*
   shiner *Cymatogaster aggregata*
Topsmelt *Atherinops affinis*
Turbot, diamond *Hypsopsetta guttulata*

Amphibians
Bullfrog *Rana catesbeiana*
Salamander, Santa Cruz long-toed *Ambystoma macrodactylum croceum*
   Pacific slender *Batrachoseps pacificus*
Toad, California *Bufo boreas halophilus*
Treefrog, Pacific *Hyla regilla*

Reptiles
Lizard, Northwestern fence *Sceloporus occidentalis occidentalis*
Snake, Monterey ringneck *Diadophis punctatus vandenburghi*
   coast garter *Thamnophis elegans terrestris*
   Pacific gopher *Pituophis melanoleucus catenifer*
Turtle, Southwestern pond *Clemmys marmorata marmorata*

Birds
Avocet, American *Recurvirostra americana*
Blackbird, red-winged *Agelaius phoeniceus*
Black-necked stilt *Himantopus mexicanus*
Bufflehead *Bucephala albeola*
Bushtit *Psaltriparus minimus*
Chickadee, chestnut-backed *Parus rufescens*
Coot, American *Fulica americana*
Curlew, long-billed *Numenius americanus*
Dowitchers *Limnodromus* spp.
Dunlin *Calidris alpina*
Eagle, golden *Aquila chrysaetos*
Egret, great *Casmerodius albus*
   snowy *Egretta thula*
Falcon, peregrine *Falco peregrinus*
Flicker, red-shafted *Colaptes auratus*
Godwit, marbled *Limosa fedoa*
Goldeneye, common *Bucephala clangula*
Grebe, eared *Podiceps nigricollis*
   Western *Aechmophorus occidentalis*
Gull, California *Larus californicus*
   Heermann's *Larus heermanni*
   Herring *Larus argentatus*
   Ring-billed *Larus delawarensis*
   Western *Larus occidentalis*
Hawk, red-tailed *Buteo jamaicensis*
Heron, great blue *Ardea herodias*
   black-crowned night *Nycticorax nycticorax*
   green-backed *Butorides striatus*
Hummingbird, Allen's *Selasphorus sasin*
Kestrel, American *Falco sparverius*
Killdeer *Charadrius vociferus*
Mallard *Anas platyrhynchos*
Meadowlark, Western *Sturnella neglecta*
Pelican, brown *Pelecanus occidentalis*
Phalarope, red-necked *Phalaropus lobatus*
Pine siskin *Carduelis pinus*
Pintail, Northern *Anas acuta*
Phoebe, black *Sayornis nigricans*
Plover, black-bellied *Pluvialis squatarola*
   semipalmated *Charadrius semipalmatus*
   snowy *Charadrius alexandrinus*
Quail, California *Callipepla californica*
Rail, clapper *Rallus longirostris*
Robin, American *Turdus migratorius*
Ruddy duck *Oxyura jamaicensis*
Ruddy turnstone *Arenaria interpres*
Sanderling *Calidris alba*
Sandpiper, least *Calidris minutilla*
   Western *Calidris mauri*
Shoveler, Northern *Anas clypeata*
Sparrow, golden-crowned *Zonotrichia atricapilla*
   Savannah *Passerculus sandwichensis*
   song *Melospiza melodia*
   white-crowned *Zonotrichia leucophrys*
Swallow, barn *Hirundo rustica*
   cliff *Hirundo pyrrhonota*
   tree *Tachycineta bicolor*
   violet-green *Tachycineta thalassina*
Teal, green-winged *Anas crecca*
   cinnamon *Anas cyanoptera*
Tern, Caspian *Sterna caspia*
   elegant *Sterna elegans*
   Forster's *Sterna forsteri*
Warbler, Wilson's *Wilsonia pusilla*
   yellow-rumped *Dendroica coronata*
Western flycatcher *Empidonax difficilis*
Whimbrel *Numenius phaeopus*
Wigeon, American *Anas americana*
Willet *Catoptrophorus semipalmatus*
Wren, marsh *Cistothorus palustris*
Yellowlegs, greater *Tringa melanoleuca*

Mammals
Cottontail, Audubon *Sylvilagus audubonii*
Coyote *Canis latrans*
Deer, mule *Odocoileus hemionus*
Harbor seal *Phoca vitulina*
Jackrabbit, blacktail *Lepus californicus*
Mouse, California meadow *Microtus californicus*
   California pocket *Perognathus californicus*
   deer *Peromyscus maniculatus*
   Western harvest *Reithrodontomys megalotis*
Muskrat *Ondatra zibethica*
Opossum *Didelphis marsupialis*
Rabbit, brush *Sylvilagus bachmani*
Raccoon *Procyon lotor*
Shrew, vagrant *Sorex vagrans*
Skunk, striped *Mephitis mephitis*
Squirrel, California ground *Spermophilus beecheyi*
   Western gray *Sciurus griseus*
Sea lion, California *Zalophus californianus*
Sea otter *Enhydra lutris*
Weasel, longtail *Mustela frenata*

INDEX